P9-ARW-894

ABC TRAVEL GUIDES FOR KIDS

PHILADELPHIA

This Guide Belongs to

_____ **Age** _____

I'm Discovering Philadelphia on _____

With _____

ISBN 0-9760047-0-4

Copyright © 2005 Matthew G. Rosenberger

Published by Matthew G. Rosenberger, One Summit Street, Philadelphia, PA 19118

ABC Travel Guides For Kids is a trademark of Matthew G. Rosenberger.

Dedicated to my Grandmother, Gaga, who taught me that "Everyday is a New Discovery."

Aa

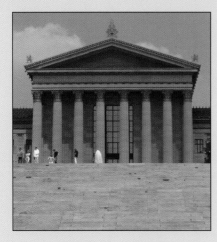

**Art Museum
Avenue of the Arts**

Bb

Broad Street

Betsy Ross House

Cc

Chinatown

Clothespin sculpture

Dd

Digging for Dinosaur Bones

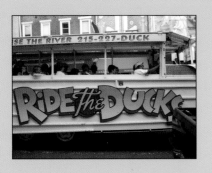

Duck Boat rides

Drexel Dragon

Ee

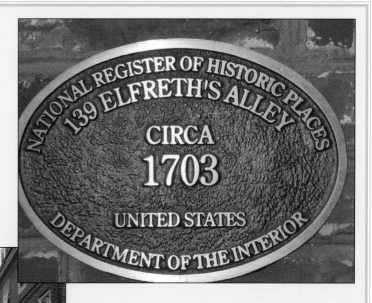

Elfreth's Alley

Ff

Fireman's Hall

Franklin Institute

Gg

Garden Railway
Display

Horticultural Center

Garden Festival
(Chestnut Hill)

Hh

Ii

Independence
Hall

Italian
Market

Jj

Japanese House & Garden

John Jenks Playground

Kimmel Center

Kk

Ll

L is for L O V E

and the Liberty Bell

Mm

Mummers

National Constitution Center

Nn

Oo

O'Doodles Toy Store

Pp

Philadelphia International Children's Festival

Pretzels

Please Touch Museum

Qq

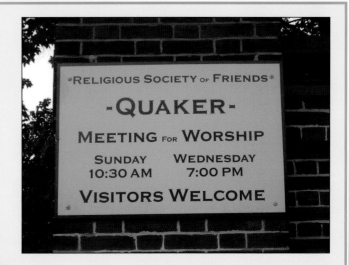

Quaker

Rr

Reading Terminal Market

Ss

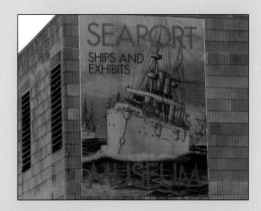

Seaport Museum

Schuylkill Center

Tt

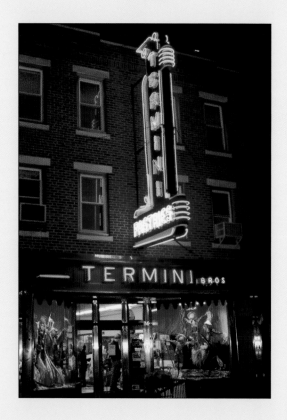

Tea Biscuits

Termini Bros. Bakery

United States Mint

Visitor Center

Ww

Water Works

Xx

X on a huge domino

Yy

Young Artists

Zz

Zooballoon

My Favorite Things in Philadelphia

_____

_____

_____

_____

_____

_____

_____

_____

Avenue of the Arts
Covering 4.1 miles of Broad Street
North from Lehigh Avenue (Temple University),
South to Washington Avenue.

Art Museum
26th Street and the Benjamin Franklin Parkway
215-763-8100
www.philamuseum.org

Betsy Ross House
239 Arch St
215-686-1252
www.betsyrosshouse.org

Chinatown Friendship Arch
10th Street and Arch Street

Clothes Pin Sculpture
15th and Market Streets

Digging for Dinosaur Bones
At The Academy of Natural Sciences
1900 Benjamin Franklin Parkway
215-299-1000
www.acnatsci.org

Drexel Dragon
33rd and Chestnut Streets

Ducks
Ride the Ducks
437 Chestnut Street
215-227-DUCK
www.phillyducks.com

Elfreth's Alley
Elfreth's Alley Museum
126 Elfreths Alley
215-574-0560
www.elfrethsalley.org

Fireman's Hall Museum
2nd and Quarry Street
215-923-1438
www.ushistory.org/tour/tour_fireman.htm

Franklin Institute
20th Street and the Benjamin Franklin Parkway
215-448-1200
www.fi.edu

Garden Railway Display
At the Morris Arboretum
100 Northwestern Avenue
215-247-5777
www.morrisarboretum.org

Garden Festival
Chestnut Hill
7600-8700 Germantown Avenue
215-247-6696
www.chestnuthillpa.com

Horticultural Center
Belmont Avenue on N. Horticultural Drive
215-685-0107
www.phila.gov/fairpark/

Independence Hall
Chestnut Street between 5th and 6th Streets
215-965-2305
www.nps.gov/inde

Italian Market
9th Street between Wharton & Christian Sts.
www.phillyitalianmarket.com

Japanese House and Garden
4700 Ohio States Drive
215-878-5097
www.shofuso.com

John Story Jenks Playground
(Chestnut Hill)
8301 Germantown Avenue

Kimmel Center
Broad and Spruce Streets
215-790-5800
www.kimmelcenter.org

Love Sculpture
Love Park
JFK and Benjamin Franklin Parkways

Liberty Bell
Liberty Bell Center
6th and Market Streets

Mummers
Mummers Museum
2nd Street and Washington
215-336-3050
www.riverfrontmummers.com/museum.html

National Constitution Center
Independence Mall
525 Arch Street
215-409-6600
www.constitutioncenter.org

O'Doodles Toy Store
8335 Germantown Avenue
215-247-7405
www.odoodles.com

Philadelphia International Children's Festival
Annenberg Center
University of Pennsylvania
3680 Walnut Street
215-898-6701
www.pennpresents.org

Please Touch Museum
210 N. 21st Street
215-963-0667
www.pleasetouchmuseum.org

Quaker
Arch Street Meeting House
320 Arch Street
215-627-2667
www.archstreetfriends.org

City Hall and Tower
Broad and Market Streets
215-686-2840
www.phila.gov

Reading Terminal Market
12th and Arch Streets
215-922-2317
www.readingterminalmarket.org

Seaport Museum
211 Columbus Boulevard
215-925-5439
www.phillyseaport.org

Schuylkill Center
8480 Hagy's Mill Road
215-482-7300
www.schuylkillcenter.org

Termini Bros. Bakery
1523 South 8th Street
215-334-1816
www.termini.com

United States Mint
Independence Mall
151 N. 5th Street
215-408-0114
www.usmint.gov

Visitor Center
6th and Markets Streets, NE Corner
215-965-7676
www.independencevisitorcenter.com

Water Works
Interpretive Center
640 Water Works Drive
215-685-4908
www.fairmountwaterworks.org

X on a huge domino
Courtyard of the Municipal Services Building
1401 JFK Boulevard

Young Artists Exhibit
School District of Philadelphia
Administration Building

Zooballoon
Philadelphia Zoo
3400 W. Girard Avenue
215-243-1100
www.philadelphiazoo.org